Mae Jemison

By Nancy Polette

Consultant
Jeanne Clidas, Ph.D.
National Reading Consultant
and
Professor of Reading, SUNY Brockport

 Children's Press ®
A Division of Scholastic Inc.
New York   Toronto   London   Auckland   Sydney
Mexico City   New Delhi   Hong Kong
Danbury, Connecticut

Designer: Herman Adler Design
Photo Researcher: Caroline Anderson
The photo on the cover shows Mae Jemison.

Library of Congress Cataloging-in-Publication Data

Polette, Nancy.
   Mae Jemison / by Nancy Polette.
      p. cm. — (Rookie biographies)
Includes index.
Summary: An introduction to the life of Mae Jemison, engineer,
physician, and astronaut.
   ISBN 0-516-22856-0 (lib. bdg.)   0-516-27783-9 (pbk.)
   1. Jemison, Mae, 1956—Juvenile literature. 2. African American
women astronauts—Biography—Juvenile literature. 3. Astronauts—
United States—Biography—Juvenile literature. [1. Jemison, Mae, 1956-
2. Astronauts. 3. Physicians. 4. Scientists. 5. African Americans—Biography.
6. Women—Biography.] I. Title. II. Series: Rookie biography.
   TL789.85.J46 P65 2003
   629.45'0092—dc21

                              2002015153

Would you like to be a star
or travel to the stars?

Mae Jemison did both. The space shuttle *Endeavour* (en-DEV-ur) blasted off on September 12, 1992. Jemison was one of the astronauts (AS-truh-nawts) on board.

She was the first African
American woman to travel in
space. She was a star!

Jemison was born in 1956 in Decatur, Alabama, but grew up in Chicago, Illinois.

Jemison liked learning new things when she was a child. She liked to read, dance, and find out how things worked.

Chicago skyscrapers

She saw the first astronauts walk on the Moon when she was 13. This made her want to be an astronaut, too.

Jemison wanted to make her dream come true. She studied hard and finished high school when she was only sixteen. She went to college to learn to be a chemical (KEM-uh-kuhl) engineer.

After college, she went to medical school and became a doctor.

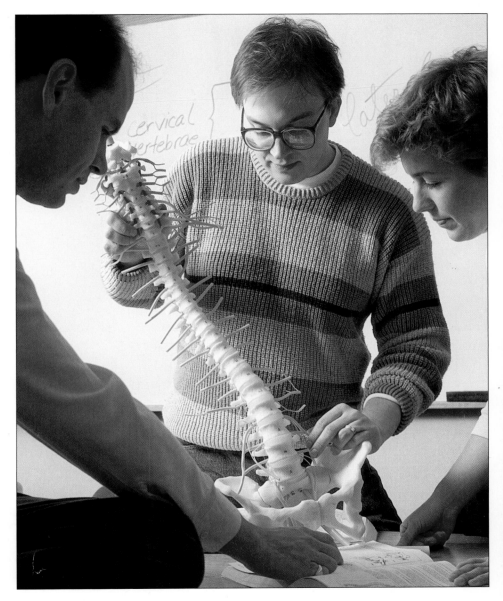

11

Peace Corps Volunteer

Jemison joined the Peace Corps when she was 26 years old. The Peace Corps sent her to Africa. She worked hard to bring medical care to poor people.

Two years later she returned to
the United States. It was time
to make her dream come true.

Kennedy Space Center

Jemison wanted to join the astronaut program. Two thousand other people wanted to join the astronaut program, too. Only fifteen people would be chosen by NASA.

Would Jemison be one of them?

Yes! NASA told Jemison she could train to be an astronaut.

17

Jemison worked hard for four years.

She learned to fly a jet.

She learned to use a parachute
(PA-ruh-shoot).

She learned how to stay alive
in wild places.

In 1992, Jemison traveled in space for eight days.

Jemison did experiments (ek-SPER-uh-ments) in space. She wanted to find a way to keep astronauts from getting sick in space. She wanted to find a way to keep their bones strong.

The shuttle went around Earth 127 times.

When Jemison looked at Earth from space, what do you think she saw? She saw Chicago, the place where her dream began.

Jemison left NASA to start her own company in 1993. She wanted to teach people in poor countries how medicine and technology (tek-NOL-uh-jee) could make their lives better.

Mae Jemison showed everyone that dreams can come true if people work to be the best that they can be.

Words You Know

Mae Jemison

astronaut

Endeavour

jet

30

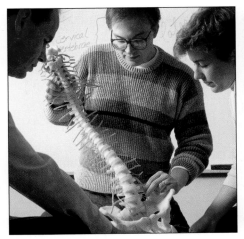

medical school

NASA

parachute

Peace Corps

31

Index

About the Author

Nancy Polette, a reading consultant and former elementary school teacher, has written both fiction and nonfiction for children, including a novel and three picture books. She lives in O'Fallon, Missouri.

Photo Credits

Photographs © 2003: Corbis Images: 28 (Marc Asnin), 7 (Bettmann), 3 (Julian Hirshowitz), 8, 30 top right (Roger Ressmeyer/NASA); NASA: cover, 4, 5, 17, 18, 20, 21, 23, 24, 30 bottom right, 30 top left, 30 bottom left, 31 bottom left; Photo Researchers, NY: 13 (David R. Frazier), 14, 31 top right (Max & Bea Hunn), 11, 31 top left (Will & Deni McIntyre), 27 (NASA/SCIENCE), 12, 31 bottom right (Elaine Rebman).